Think Up!

An anthology of short articles to help achieve a positive mindset

By Mark Arsenault

Think Up!

An anthology of short articles to help achieve a positive mindset

By Mark Arsenault

Gold Rush Publishing
GoldRushPub.com
Elk Grove, CA

Think Up! An anthology of short articles to help achieve a positive mindset
Copyright © 2016 by Mark T. Arsenault.
Published by Gold Rush Publishing.

Gold Rush Publishing
PO Box 582155
Elk Grove, CA 95758
916-572-4478
E-mail: goldrushpub@gmail.com

www.GoldRushPub.com

Think Up! is a trademark owned by Mark T. Arsenault.

Visit **MarkTruth.com** for free inspirational, motivational and instructional material.

Cover design by Mark T. Arsenault

Cover illustration: ClipArt.com. Used under license.

ISBN: 978-1-890305-16-1 paperback

Printed in USA

Contents

Dedication

This book is dedicated to all of the teachers, spiritual leaders, and mentors I have had through my life.

Every time I speak to a group or record a video, my audience sees only me. But, as the legendary speaker George Zalucki taught me, that is an illusion. What you don't see are the books I've read, the teachers I've learned from, the mentors and influences in my life that you can't see that have influenced *me* so that I may share what I have learned in an attempt to influence *you*.

When doors are closed, keep the faith

Late last year I filed the paperwork to officially create GAATES, Inc., a nonprofit organization with a mission to "help ex-offenders through personal development, career readiness, and success strategies." I joined forces with five other like-minded go-getters (including two pastors, a peace officer, an educator, and a business leader). While not a faith-based organization, we created the organization in faith.

We applied for and received 501(c)(3) tax-exempt status from the IRS! My faith was strong at that point, to be sure! Everything was a go and we were going to hold a big event to raise money to launch the nonprofit in a big way.

We were ready to go, that is, until I was told by my employer that what I wanted to do with my nonprofit was too similar to what they were already paying other organizations to do and it could be perceived as a conflict of interest. That created a situation where I could be considered in violation of my employer's (overly vague, in my opinion) policy. So, in short, I inferred that I could not help ex-offenders through my nonprofit as long as I was employed by an agency that paid entities to help offenders and ex-offenders.

My faith was a bit shaken but still strong. My vision was a powerful one and I knew it would come to pass. But in the here and now, I had a choice to make.

I could:

1. Push forward and risk being disciplined, up to and including the possibility of being terminated (thus losing 20 years of work toward my retirement)

2. Quit my job (losing much of said retirement contributions); or

3. Put the nonprofit on hold until I left my current employ (i.e., retired).

The first and second options didn't seem prudent, so I opted for number three. I also lost four of my founding directors in the process. (Some people are very nervous about potential legal threats.)

Was I upset? No. Disappointed, yes, but not really upset. My vision for what I'm going to do with my nonprofit organization is too big to be threatened by this. This is just a bump in the road. I have faith that what God has put in my heart will come to pass, exactly as it's supposed to. When doors — or in this case GAATES — seem to be shut tight, trust that He will open another one, exactly where and when it's supposed to open.

So for the time being, I continue to give 100% at work and I continue to keep my eye on the big picture. That's something we all should do.

Think of a time a door closed on you.

How did it make you feel?

_____

_____

_____

_____

How did you react?

_____

_____

_____

_____

Could you have reacted differently?

_____

_____

_____

_____

What new doors opened as a result?

_____

_____

_____

_____

It's Not the Goal That Drives You

Have you ever considered why you are doing something and thought, "Well, that's a silly question. I want to do it for such-and-so" ("such-and-so" being the seemingly obvious goal)?

Consider that the "obvious" answer isn't the real answer at all. Here's what I mean.

The goals we set for ourselves are real, but they're not the real reasons we do what we do. We do what we do not because of the goal but rather because of what achieving the goal will do for us. In other words, it's not the benefits of doing the thing that drive us. It's the benefit of the benefit of doing the thing that drives us.

Here's an example. Why do most of us go to work at a job? The answer is obvious, right? We work for money. We work to get paid, right? Wrong. We work so that we can acquire money (the benefit) so that we can pay our bills (the benefit of the benefit). Ultimately, we work so that we can pay our bills.

Here's another example. Why do we buy flowers on Valentine's Day? We buy flowers to give to that special person in our life to make them happy, right? Wrong. We buy flowers to give to that special person in our life to make them happy (the benefit) for what it does for our relationship with them (the benefit of the benefit).

So the next time you consider why you (or someone else) is doing something, consider the real, underlying reason. Consider the benefit of the benefit because that's what truly drives human beings. There's an illustration that was used in a sales training book I once read. It went like this:

People don't go to the hardware store with the goal of buying a drill. They go to the hardware store because they need to make a hole. That makes sense, doesn't it? Nobody really "needs" a drill. What they need are the holes that a drill makes. That's the benefit of the benefit.

So the next time you are looking for a reason to do something, or even a reason to persuade someone else to do something, consider the benefit of the benefit. What will doing that thing really accomplish for you (or them)?

If we focus on the benefit, that alone might not outweigh the perceived negatives of doing something. If that's the case, we won't do it. For example, if I work out I will lose some fat and get in better shape. Is that enough of a motivator for me to go exercise, get all sweaty and feel pain? Absolutely not. But if I consider what losing weight and being fit will do for me, such as allowing me to fit into a nice suit I want to buy, give me more energy and a longer life to spend with my children, then it absolutely is worth the pain and sweat.

It's not the benefit of the exercise alone that motivates, but the benefit of the benefit that drives us to do what we do.

Think of a goal you've set.

What's a benefit of achieving that goal?

_____

_____

_____

_____

What's a benefit of achieving the benefit?

_____

_____

_____

_____

Is the goal or the benefit more exciting?

_____

_____

_____

_____

Name other goals you might re-examine.

_____

_____

_____

_____

Sometimes you need to be spontaneous and visit the ocean

A couple of Saturdays ago, my wife told me once again she was feeling out of sorts and wanted to visit the ocean. "I love the ocean. I just want to go back, see it, stand in it, and get some perspective. The ocean is my place to go when I feel like this."

She'd mentioned the ocean a couple times in the week prior, so when I heard her say it again Saturday morning I knew she was intent on going. The closest beach is a lake but that clearly wouldn't do. She wanted to visit the ocean. The nearest ocean beach is almost two-hours from our house by car. Should we go?

Why not? It sounded like a good idea to me, so we put our shoes on and hopped into the car for a cruise down to the Bay Area and the ocean. Just like that. You see, back in the day I was never one for spontaneous acts like that but these days, after surviving cancer and losing my mother a few years ago, I've learned the value of being spontaneous.

We didn't have a particular beach in mind. Once we got to San Francisco we simply did a search for "beach" on the GPS. It's kind of funny but we ended up at a beach called "The Beach" on the edge of The City. After a bit of a struggle parking, we headed down to the water.

There were a lot of people there and we met come really great people, like Mike and Mel, a great couple from the East Bay who brought their dog down for some exercise.

We walked up and down the beach as our daughter ran in the surf, chasing dogs and ducking kite strings. The sound of the waves breaking reminded me of our recent vacation in New England, and the cool sea air was quite refreshing. It was a great experience for all of us. More importantly, we spent time together as a family and created a memory.

We didn't get back home until very late that night. We were exhausted (actually, I was the only one still awake, which is a good thing because I was driving) but it was worth every minute and I'm glad we went.

It would have been easy to say "No way. It's too far to drive for just a few hours on the coast," but that would have been missing the point. Life is too short to not do the things you want to do. To intentionally skip an opportunity to have an experience – to have fun – is to waste the gift that life is.

When you get an opportunity to create a memory, to live life, and you hear that voice in your head telling you all of the reasons not to do it, stop and think about the reasons why you should do it. Will it make you happy? Will it make someone else happy? Will it create a positive memory? Is it possible you'll never get the opportunity again?

Don't just think of the negative. Think of the positive. Live life. Go to the ocean more often.

Consider your outlook on spontaneity.

Name a situation that could have improved by you being spontaneous.

_____

_____

_____

If you could relive the experience, would you do it differently? Why or why not?

_____

_____

_____

Name three advantages of being spontaneous?

_____

_____

_____

How can you be more spontaneous in the future?

_____

_____

_____

_____

Sometimes life just sucks – get over it & keep moving forward

It's true. No matter what your mindset, sometimes life throws you a curve ball and you have to deal with some challenging circumstance. That's a nice way of saying that sometimes life just sucks. Life can beat you down and leaves you curled up on the ground wondering what happened. It's not a matter of whether or not it will happen. It will happen. What matters in how you respond.

> **"...sometimes life throws you a curve ball and you have to deal with some challenging circumstance. That's a nice way of saying that sometimes life just sucks."**

It's easy to take the licking and give up on whatever endeavor led you to that result. That's broke thinking. Broke as in "having lack" – lack of finances, lack of work ethic, lack of maturity... The average person takes a hit from life and decides what they're doing is hard and gives up, perhaps even on life itself. Average people do not anticipate life's blows and so when they come, they are mentally unprepared. Negative self-talk including "Life just sucks," is literal self-sabotage.

How can you turn life's tragedies into your triumphs? Be prepared.

The successful mindset dictates that we anticipate bad things will happen and prepare for them, mentally or otherwise. That's not to say that we live in depression and defeat. Far from it. Knowing that life can – and will – hit hard, we can decide ahead of time what meaning we will assign to events and how we will respond to them.

Have you noticed that the best leaders typically stay calm in the face of adversity? Why is that? It's because they prepared themselves for how to handle adversity. They know the importance of making a decision and taking action when facing one of life's haymakers, while others are panicking.

Tony Robbins said, "Things do not have meaning. We assign meaning to everything." What does this mean? It means that when something happens to us, it's up to us to decide what meaning that event has. We have the ability to find some good for ourselves, perhaps not from the event itself but as a result of the event.

"Things do not have meaning. We assign meaning to everything." – Tony Robbins

Here's an example. A few years ago my mother passed away after a short but terminal illness. I went into depression for a time. I described it as being able to live and laugh each day but having no sense of my own future. I compared my lack of vision to looking into the future and seeing only a mist or fog. I had no sense of future. Over time, through personal development, I changed my belief and assigned a new meaning to her death.

Today, while I still miss her terribly, I celebrate her life and remain grateful for all of the positive things she gave me, and I made a decision to grow and become more than I ever had before. Reaching for my full potential was a way I could honor her. The good that came from her passing was my decision to get involved in personal development.

"You have to come to your closed doors before you get to your open doors…" – Joel Osteen

Joel Osteen, pastor of Lakewood Church, had this to say about setbacks in an interview:

"You have to come to your closed doors before you get to your open doors… What if you knew you had to go through 32 closed doors before you got to your open door? Well, then you'd come to closed door number eight and you'd think, 'Great, I got another one out of the way'… Keep moving forward. You're learning from them and you're one step closer to the open door."

The next time you are facing a tough circumstance, know that that event does not define you. Your destiny, your potential is so much more. Everything we experience is for our benefit, in terms of providing us an opportunity to grow. Remember, too, when we are in our greatest need, one way to receive is to give to others. An attitude of gratitude, giving and moving forward can carry us through any hardship.

Sometimes life just sucks, plain and simple. There will always be challenges.

The opposite is also true. Sometimes life is wonderful. There will always be successes and joy. As long as you know in advance you can prepare your mind for how you will respond to each and, most importantly, keep moving forward.

Think of a tragedy or major disappointment you've experienced.

What meaning did you assign the event?

_____

_____

_____

_____

What other meaning could it have?

_____

_____

_____

_____

What is something positive that came of it?

_____

_____

_____

What other circumstances are "doors" you have to go through to reach your goal?

_____

_____

_____

_____

The difference between external belief and internal belief

Before I even I started my business I had strong belief in the company and the products. I had belief that others could be – and were being – successful in the company. But I hit a block. I was not seeing success, initially, and I couldn't figure out why.

After some soul searching and personal development, I learned that what I lacked was personal belief. I knew others could have success but I didn't have belief that I could have the same success. My external belief was extremely high. My internal belief, however, was low.

The issue wasn't with the company or the products and services it offered. The documentation on the company was (and remains) irrefutable. The company's been written about in a virtual "Who's Who" of business publications. I saw and heard enough to know that the company was a strong one, studied the compensation plan and knew it was solid, and I saw people who were successful and making good money in the business. I knew the products and services offered by the company were top notch, provided by major suppliers also with well-known names and excellent reputations. There was no doubt that everything was in place to run a very successful and lucrative business.

So what was the problem? The problem, frankly, was me. I didn't have the level of belief in myself. My internal belief was weak. This took me some months to realize, after a significant amount of personal development and growth.

Maybe you're in that place I was in when it comes to a goal or project you're involved in. "Sure, other people have done it," you may tell yourself, "but that doesn't mean that I'm good enough. It doesn't mean that I can be that successful."

I've got news for you. If you're listening to that kind of self-talk, you're being lied to! Andy Andrews what said, "Don't believe everything you think!"

The fact of the matter is that whatever someone else can accomplish, you can accomplish, too… if you commit yourself to not only doing what it takes but also to becoming who you need to become. That's it. "Whatever it takes" needs to become your mantra.

Know that you have everything you need to reach your dream. Even if your internal belief is low, like mine was, you can accomplish whatever you want in life.

All you have to do is:

- Decide to accomplish it
- Commit to doing whatever it takes, and
- Become the person you need to become to reach your goals.

You can do it. I have faith in you.

Your External vs. Internal Belief.

What is a situation in which your external belief is high but your internal belief is low?

_____

_____

_____

Name people who have achieved the goal.

_____

_____

_____

_____

List reasons why you _could_ reach the goal.

_____

_____

_____

_____

What's a step you can take tomorrow to help reach your goal?

_____

_____

_____

_____

Stop praying and take a look around you

Have you been praying for something for a while? Stop for a moment and look around in your life. Don't look for what you want to happen but what He might have put in your life that answers the prayer.

When we focus on what we want we're more likely to find it. That's our reticular activating system at work. At the same time, however, by focusing on what we want we tend to miss the things we aren't looking for.

When it comes to opportunities, we often miss them because we're too focused on what we want instead of what we might need.

Think outside the box. Prayers are often answered with the "means" we need rather than the "end" we desire.

In the movie *Evan Almighty*, there's a scene in which God (playing a waiter) talks with Evan's wife in a diner. His dialogue is worth thinking about. In the film, he says;

"If someone prays for patience, do you think God gives them patience or do you think God gives them the opportunity to be patient? If they pray for courage does God give them courage or do you think God gives them the opportunity to be courageous? If someone prayed for their family to be closer, do you think God zaps them with warm fuzzy feelings or does he give them opportunities to love each other?"

It's one of them best motivational scenes on film, in my humble opinion. Here's what it illustrates for me:

Stop praying for a moment and look around for your reply. God has already provided you with everything you need to achieve greatness. You just have to see it and put it to use.

Think about what you're praying for.

What are you praying for?

_____

_____

_____

_____

How can your prayer be answered?

_____

_____

_____

_____

How might your prayer already have been answered?

_____

_____

_____

_____

What new opportunities do you now see?

_____

_____

_____

_____

To increase your success, you must attend events

There's a saying that "success leaves clues," meaning that others have had great success and we can, too, by simply doing what they've done. There are a number of things that we need to focus on in order to see that success. One of them is belief. In my mindset seminars I talk about the "success cycle": Belief, Expectations, Actions, and Results, and back to Belief.

- **Belief** – what we believe, our core values – determines our expectations
- **Expectations** influence our actions (i.e., our level of effort and commitment)
- **Actions** lead to results
- **Results** tend to reinforce our belief.

If our belief is shaky, we don't expect good results, which typically leads to little action, which leads to poor results, which just reinforces our belief. The cool thing is that the same works in reverse! If our belief is strong, we expect good results, which leads to much more action, which leads to those good results we expected, which reinforces our belief. The cycle can work for you or against you. It all depends on your level of belief.

"The cycle can work for you or against you. It all depends on your level of belief."

So what are some ways to build your belief? One of the best ways I know is to attend events. These events can be seminars in which you go listen to one or more speakers, or perhaps organizational events, such as an event put on by your company or organization, like a sports team. The goal of the kind of events I'm referring to is to increase your belief in whatever thing it is you're doing.

As you may know, among my many ventures I'm also a network marketing professional. I recently attended one of our company's events on the East Coast. The best way I can describe it is three days of intense training, personal development and belief-building in a concert environment.

I got to spend time with more than 20,000 other people with whom I share the same long term vision and goals, I got to hear incredibly inspirational stories from people who've done what I'm doing, I got to meet celebrities and notable people who either endorse or are in my business, and I got some absolutely first-rate training from leadership expert John C. Maxwell. And I got all that for less than $200. That's an absolute steal, my friends. Just one hour with John C. Maxwell would cost you many times that amount.

The quality of each experience is going to vary, but what you take away from the event is up to you. In my case, the experience was easily worth ten times as much as I paid to attend. The energy of 20,000 people who are all excited about the same things I'm excited about will boost your belief (it's referred to as "social proof"). I am so convinced of the necessity – yes necessity – of these events for my success that I attend at least two major, international training events a year, sometimes as many as four a year, plus several regional events, and regular local events.

"The quality of each experience is going to vary, but what you take away from the event is up to you."

And that doesn't even include non-company-specific events, such as the *Success* symposium I attended last year, where I got to see and listen to speakers like Les Brown. You can ask anyone on my team; I am a huge proponent of events. In fact, I'm at an event today!

I'm telling you, if you want to increase your belief in order to have greater success in whatever it is that you're doing, you need to attend events. Period.

So start looking for these events that can boost your belief. If you're not in network marketing, like I am, you can look for motivational speaker events, faith-based events, training events, social networking events... whatever it is that applies to your goals and your dreams. Just get there. Your life will never be the same.

Consider an area where you lack belief.

List some local events related to the topic.

_____

_____

_____

_____

Is there a meet-up group related to the topic?

_____

_____

_____

_____

Is there an online course related to the topic?

_____

_____

_____

_____

Where else can you find social proof?

_____

_____

_____

_____

Change the people who are around you

My wife came home recently, as cheerful and energetic as I've seen her in months. She'd recently sought out and joined a local *MeetUp* group for successful women. She went straight to the event after work while I stayed home and took care of the house. She was gone several hours, so I knew she was having a good time.

When she walked through the door she had a big smile on her face. She was radiating energy like I haven't seen in weeks. After putting her things down and saying goodnight to our daughter (who'd been in bed for a while), she sat down to tell me all about her evening. She excitedly told me about each of the women she met, telling me each one's name and what she learned about them. As each of the women introduced herself at the meet-up, my wife told me, she took notes. She practiced each woman's name each time she spoke to them. Now that's taking networking seriously!

She continued to describe the event but what she really focused on was the people she met. She was genuinely excited about meeting and spending time with a group of like-minded people, describing them as "refreshing" and "inspiring." She told me what a difference it is being around positive women who want to grow as people, compared to many of her co-workers who are unhappy with their circumstances but have settled for mediocrity. She proclaimed she is going to spend more time with her new friends and, in fact, seek out more like-minded people to add to her circle of new friends. That's putting the power of association to good use!

I put the same power to work in my own life by choosing to associate with people more successful than me, as well as people who will encourage me in my growth. I recently attended a huge company training event for my business. I spent three days with my team and 20,000 other like-minded people in a rock concert environment of training and personal growth, topped off by hearing the legendary John. C. Maxwell speak live and in person. It was absolutely phenomenal.

I'm minimizing my association with negative people, if not cutting them out altogether. I just don't have time to spend being dragged down emotionally and psychologically. My future and my goals are too important for that, and I will never accomplish those goals if I allow myself to be poisoned by people with a negative mindset, no matter how well-intentioned they may be.

Look, many of the people we know are negative. They're stuck in their lives and they don't see things getting any better. Negative people don't believe their lives can improve much so they don't bother trying. They settle for mediocrity and tell themselves that they're content with lack. Because of that mindset, anything we do to improve our own lives acts as a mirror to the negative people. They'll get uncomfortable when you refuse to settle for average. Why? Because your desire reminds them of what they're not doing. Often times, they will start to criticize your efforts, make fun of you or mock you, or tell you that what you're doing is pointless, selfish, or any of a hundred other things intended to get you to quit.

I'm here to tell you... Don't quit! Nothing worth having was ever easy to accomplish. If you truly want to make a positive change in your life you have to change! Jim Rohn said it well when he said, "Life doesn't get better by chance. It gets better by choice." Make the choice to change your life and then change it. One area you can change that may be more important than any other is your associations.

"Life doesn't get better by chance. It gets better by choice."

Don't settle for mediocrity, my friend. You deserve better. You deserve to be happy. As the great speaker Les brown says... You have greatness within you! Now find it and let it out.

Think about who you spend time with.

Who is encouraging you, challenging you to excel, or otherwise enriching your life?

_____

_____

_____

_____

Who should you spend *less* time with? Why?

_____

_____

_____

_____

List three ways you can meet new people:

_____

_____

_____

_____

Where can you meet like-minded people?

_____

_____

_____

_____

Times have changed but the choices are still yours to make

After a top notch training event for my business this morning, I took the family to Gold Rush Days this afternoon for some family fun time.

Gold Rush Days is a weekend-long event held in historic Old Sacramento with lots of vendors, Old West-themed events (both historic and anachronistic) and more. The streets are closed to motor vehicle traffic and covered with literally tons of dirt.

We also went on a wagon ride, saw a plethora Gold Rush era reenactors, visited the old historic school house, ate some delicious food and met some terrific people. On the wagon ride we were passing in front of the cannon when it was fired. Okay, it was about 100 yards away but it was still extremely loud and startled more than a few people, including my daughter! Overall, however, the day was a great success.

One of the things I took away from the day was how much our society has changed in just over 100 years and yet how little human beings have changed in terms of our psychology. In the Gold Rush era letters were carried by stagecoach (and later by young men on horseback) over thousands of miles, only to be replaced by the telegraph.

Today we can instantly communicate with people on the other side of the world via video teleconferencing. Despite advances in technology, however, people today still deal with the same mental and emotional struggles as their ancestors. Doubt, fear, and poor self-confidence still rob people of the success they deserve. In some ways technology actually exacerbates the problem. We're bombarded with an overwhelming amount of information, most of it negative and intended to instill artificial expectations and shape our beliefs as consumers.

At the same time, however, we can use technology to our advantage. If we decide to focus on the positive and engage in personal growth, our resources are virtually limitless, especially in contrast to the days reenacted during the Gold Rush Days. We still maintain the ability to choose what we allow into our minds. We can limit our TV viewing, reading, music and other media to those things that will enrich our lives…if we choose to. We're closer than ever before, despite any distance between us, yet we can still choose who we associate with. There are more choices to be made today than ever before but they are still our choices to make.

Proverbs 4:23 cautions us to "Guard your heart above all else, for it determines the course of your life." Choose carefully what you expose your mind – and your heart – to. You are the final arbiter of what you watch, read, listen to and who you associate with. These are the things that will affect your beliefs more than anything else.

Enjoy your family and enjoy your life. And above all else, guard your heart.

Consider the technology today.

List three ways technology benefits you:

_____

_____

_____

_____

What technology could you use less of?

_____

_____

_____

_____

How could you use 4 extra hours a week?

_____

_____

_____

_____

List three sources of positivity in your day.

_____

_____

_____

_____

What the 54th Mass. taught me about success

One hundred fifty years ago, Union Army Colonel Robert Gould Shaw and 272 soldiers of the 54th Massachusetts Infantry, perhaps the most famous regiment of African-American troops during the war, were killed in an assault on Fort Wagner, near Charleston, South Carolina. The approach to Fort Wagner was a fifty-foot-wide strip of beach, with the Atlantic Ocean on one side and swampy marshland on the other. Shaw and the 54th Massachusetts, and other Union regiments, managed to penetrate the 600-foot-wide walls at two points but didn't have sufficient numbers to take the fort. By the end of the battle, there were more than 1,500 Union soldiers that became casualties or were taken prisoner (compared to the Confederates' 222).

Imagine what was going through the minds of those Union soldiers, the smell of gunpowder. The sounds of the surf, gunshots and exploding shells. Even though they knew it was likely a suicide mission, there was a greater cause for which they fought. Something larger than themselves compelled them to fight on against overwhelming odds. Although the battle (which was immortalized in the 1990 motion picture Glory, starring Mathew Broderick and Denzel Washington, who won an *Academy Award*® for his role) was a failure for the Union, it illustrates the amazing feats that human beings are capable of accomplishing.

"Gonna come a time when we all gonna hafta ante up."

Sometimes the goals and objectives we set before ourselves seem insurmountable. They seem virtually impossible. But that belief comes from negative self-talk. The fact of the matter is that human beings throughout history have accomplished great things throughout history. No matter how great the "mountain" that stands before you, know that other people have moved larger mountains, overcome larger obstacles, than the one you are facing today. How did they do it?

They did it by believing and by having a powerful reason "why." A great man once said, "If your 'why' is powerful enough, the 'how' doesn't matter." It's time to reach down inside, to visualize what you want and understand why you want it. Write it down. Turn your sporadic thoughts and wishes into a detailed paper explaining your vision and what it means to you. Create a success board, with pictures depicting what you wish to have, who you wish to be, where you wish to live, and who you wish to impact. Make your vision of tomorrow real for you today.

I imagine that many of the soldiers of the 54th Massachusetts believed they were fighting for a righteous cause – freedom. The freedom to be given an opportunity to prove themselves. Freedom to make a better life for themselves, their families, and for their future generations. I imagine their vision of the future was a very powerful one. So powerful that they were willing to fight for it and to literally lay down their lives so that one day their vision would become a reality, if not for them then for their descendants.

In *Glory*, Colonel Shaw wrote in a letter to his mother, "We fight for men and women whose poetry is not yet written but which will presently be as enviable and as renowned as any."

"We fight for men and women whose poetry is not yet written but which will presently be as enviable and as renowned as any."

By embracing your "why" and having a clear and compelling vision for the future, you will be able to charge down that narrow path and ultimately accomplish your goals, despite every distraction, nay-sayer, fear and self-doubt. Talk to that prospective client. Do that presentation. Connect with that mentor. Start that fitness program. Enroll in that class. Do those things you were once afraid to do.

Commit to achieving your goals and go after them. Decide to plant your flag and go get it, and don't let anything stand in your way. Make the achieving of your goals and dreams a "must" instead of a "should." Before long, as you start to see small successes along your journey, you'll realize that the mountain you're facing today isn't nearly as big as you once thought it was.

This column is in no way meant to minimize or diminish the sacrifices of those soldiers. Just the opposite. They were willing to pay the ultimate price so that others could live in the world they envisioned. They are true heroes and their actions should inspire others. I know they inspire me. Each time I'm in Boston I visit the monument to the 54th Massachusetts near Boston Common. I feel a great sense of gratitude for their sacrifice, both as a veteran who's experienced war and as a citizen who has benefitted from the freedoms they helped secure for me.

I encourage you to find your own inspiration. Whatever it takes for you to resolve to win. You deserve to win.

Think about a goal and your 'Why.'

What's your motivation for hitting the goal?

_____

_____

_____

_____

What happens if you *don't* reach your goal?

_____

_____

_____

Visualize reaching your goal. Describe in detail how it looks, sounds, feels & smells:

_____

_____

_____

_____

What will you put on your success board?

_____

_____

_____

_____

Diversity is key to growth and happiness

In our business, my wife and I sometimes have to split our attendance at training events. Today she attended a first class training event while I spent time with our daughter. My wife recorded the event and took great notes, so I was able to get the same great training after the fact, albeit second hand.

For some "daddy-daughter time" we went to the local multicultural festival. It turned out to be a great event for several reasons. The festival itself, in its second year, is our city's premier community-wide celebration of diversity. Thousands of people attended this popular event, which featured ethnic entertainment, food, and exhibits representing the city's diverse community. I am grateful that the city puts this event on each year, and I certainly plan to attend next year, as well.

When I first mentioned the idea my daughter was not interested in going.

"Meh," was the response, uttered with a shrug of her shoulders. Clearly I hadn't provided enough information to her for her to make an informed "yes" decision. I decided to paint a picture for her so she knew what she'd be missing if we *didn't* go.

"Imagine walking across the park," I told her, "on the soft grass, with the smell of all kinds of delicious food in the air." She raised an eyebrow. "Imagine hearing a lot of kids laughing and having fun, throwing *Frisbees* and playing in the bounce house," I continued.

"There's going to be a *bounce house?*" she asked.

"Of course!" I said. "There will probably be at least one bounce house and lots of people, all having fun. And ice cream! They're sure to have ice cream there." Her eyes were wide with interest now. "Think about what we'll miss if we don't go."

Before I knew it she had her sandals on and was shouting, "Daddy, come on! We don't want to miss it! Let's go. And bring money for ice cream!"

Once there it was almost exactly as I'd described. We found the bounce houses (both of them), along with face-painting at the Amazing Face Designs booth (where my daughter got a fantastic lavender cat face), a snow cone vender, phenomenal authentic Polish cuisine by Goasia's European Catering, and booths staffed by volunteers representing an amazing array of non-profit and grass roots organizations.

I was impressed by the sense of community and took advantage of the opportunity to meet people I'd never met before. There are so many people in just my local area, each of them with different backgrounds and different stories to tell, and each of them with something amazing to share with the world.

I could have literally spent all day there just taking with people and learning about them. I made efforts to meet as many people as I could in the short time that we were there and I'm richer for it.

You will never regret connecting with people. If you're like I was, it may be uncomfortable to "break out of your shell" and talk to people but it's well worth it. I believe that diversity is key to growth and happiness; diversity of culture, of style, of thoughts and beliefs.

You don't have to subscribe to every view or belief out there, but understanding sure makes it a lot easier to engage with people and develop a relationship with them. And by engaging with others you learn about them, their culture and, ultimately, about yourself. I know I did.

Be open to learning about new cultures.

How can you share your culture with others?

_____

_____

_____

_____

Name another culture you're interested in:

_____

_____

_____

What are some traits you share with a friend from another culture?

_____

_____

_____

_____

How has diversity improved your life?

_____

_____

_____

_____

Live life like a NASCAR driver

It's a fact that everyone's life will come to an end. It's just a matter of time. So why do so many people go through life without going after what Darren Hardy calls "those big fat hairy audacious goals?" Life's too damned short not to accomplish something great, to experience exhilaration and joy, and to live a full life.

A few weeks ago, for my birthday, my wife surprised me with a fantastic birthday present. She took me to the Stockton 99 Raceway to the Race with Rusty NASCAR Experience. I got the full treatment, complete with a short racing class, suited up in the fire suit and helmet, and got (tightly) buckled into a 3,000-pound rocket on wheels.

This was the first time in my life I'd ever been inside a *bonafide* NASCAR spec late model racing car. There's so much to know out on the track: what the different colored flags mean, what to do (and not do) in an emergency, where the track lights are and what they mean, and so on. The neck brace and head stabilizer made it almost impossible to turn your head to look at anything except the front windshield.

"That's okay. All you have to worry about is what's in front of you," I was told. "The spotter will take watch out for what's behind you." I have to tell you; I have a whole new respect for professional drivers.

To be honest with you, the moment the crewman walked away from my car and I gave a big thumbs-up out the window, I started to get very anxious. What if I lose control of the car? What if I hit a wall? Why am I here? In fact, for just a second I thought maybe I should get out of the car and call it off.

Then common sense took hold of me. Why in the world would I want to miss the opportunity of a lifetime, to skip a chance to drive on an actual NASCAR racetrack?! So I stayed.

I stayed not because I wasn't nervous. I was *still* nervous. I stayed because of how I knew I would feel after it was over: flowing with adrenaline and happy as hell that I had the memory!

That's how we should live life. Not without caution but with a longing to experience things we've never experienced before. To be able to look back and say, "Boy, I'm glad I did it." We should live life like a NASCAR driver.

You can check out a video I put together of my day at the track that I posted on my blog at MarkTruth.com. I'm glad I did it.

Are you living like a NASCAR driver?

What new experience(s) are you afraid to try?

_____

_____

_____

_____

How would it feel to do that thing?

_____

_____

_____

_____

Name three benefits of trying the new thing:

_____

_____

_____

_____

Who might be inspired by you doing it?

_____

_____

_____

_____

Stop chasing and start changing

Not long ago I came to a realization. I have been doing personal development since last summer, consuming as many books and articles, audio programs and videos as I can get my hands on. There are some fairly common messages among them, which leads one to believe that either all of these writers and speakers are involved in a common, well-orchestrated conspiracy to scam the rest of the world... or that they all know what they're talking about when it comes to achieving success.

I believe it's the latter.

One of the common themes I've been observing is that in order for you to be successful you have to undergo personal growth in *multiple* areas. That is, everyone has a handful of aspects. Here are the "big four": the physical, the mental, the spiritual, and the emotional aspects. In order to achieve your greatest potential you need to achieve growth in all four of these areas.

I don't want to linger too long on this point. What's important to relate in this article is that I have been exploring and growing in all four of these aspects. One of the things I came to realize is that each individual person, regardless of circumstance, has great personal power within them and the only reason people *don't* unleash this power is either because they don't know or don't believe they have it.

When you consider that we are the only true obstacle to our own success, one has to acknowledge that the reverse is also true. We have the ability to achieve whatever it is we believe and set out to achieve. Nothing can stop us. If a situation arises to make something physically impossible, you can't say "Well that won't work so I'm giving up." Successful people find a way over or around the obstacle.

Now, this may require them to redefine their specific goal so they can achieve their general goal but the important thing is that they persist. Success depends on consistent action toward achieving the goal. How and why you persist is not the point of this column, but you can do it if you choose.

Tony Robbins said, "I believe life is constantly testing us for our level of commitment, and life's greatest rewards are reserved for those who demonstrate a never-ending commitment to act until they achieve. This level of resolve can move mountains, but it must be constant and consistent. As simplistic as this may sound, it is still the common denominator separating those who live their dreams from those who live in regret."

I've heard it over and over again that we can do whatever we choose to do, that it simply requires action on our part. I believed that principle, of course. Why wouldn't I? It makes all the sense in the world. The problem was, I didn't really believe it for myself until now.

So many people are looking outward for the "magic bullet" that will put them on the path toward success. They are chasing success, which is unobtainable.

The legendary Jim Rohn, known as a business philosopher and a huge proponent of personal development, said, "Success is not a doing process, it is a becoming process. What you do, what you pursue, will allude you — it can be like chasing butterflies. Success is something you attract by the person you become."

The ability – the power – to achieve success is not outside of us. It's within us.

Instead of reaching outward to try to grab that power, we need to work on ourselves to unleash it. When I really got this concept, an image from a video game flashed in my mind (the game was Infamous). It just made sense. These kinds of life-changing realizations are often so incredibly simple once we "get it."

Find your personal power.

What's something you desire but don't think you can accomplish or have?

_____

_____

_____

_____

Name three people who have achieved it:

_____

_____

_____

_____

If it were possible, how would you do it?

_____

_____

_____

_____

If you couldn't fail, what would you try?

_____

_____

_____

Detail your life

My baby was looking a little sluggish so I decided to give her a bath. You should have seen her perk up! She was so excited she could barely sit still to get washed. I managed to finish her up, though.

Now she's acting like a diva. "Do my tires. Do my headlight lenses. Detail my interior!" But I love her. She deserves to get pampered now and then.

So do you.

When was the last time you treated yourself to something special? I'm not talking about dinner and a movie. I'm talking about a massage or spa treatment, getting away for a weekend in a resort, or even just spending some quiet time in a beautiful place reflecting.

Recharging is important. Success isn't all "Go! Go! Go!" You have to stop once in a while and take stock of where you are and what you've learned. Reflection is an essential part of personal development and personal growth.

"You gotta reset your sail now and then," as Jim Rohn might say.

Nothing helps reset your sail like taking the time to detail your own life.

Think about what recharges you.

What makes you feel refreshed & energized?

_____

_____

_____

_____

When was the last time you did it?

_____

_____

_____

_____

What is your ideal vacation?

_____

_____

_____

_____

How can you reward yourself for reaching milestones?

_____

_____

_____

Go for it! Take the time to do something for someone else

Sometimes in life you have to just go for it! Today is one of those days.

For an early birthday gift my wife arranged for me to have a day off from work and set up a special out-of-town event for me. I'm going to be doing something I've never done before and I can hardly wait. I'll post a video later – in the next day or so – to share what is no doubt going to be an amazing and exciting day!

The fact that my wife did something special for me is wonderful, to be sure. What means the most is the time, effort and thought that went into it. She contacted a mutual friend and explained what she wanted to do. That friend made the connection with a decision-maker at my work who gave the needed approvals. All of this occurred without me knowing about it. How cool is that?

You can do the same thing for someone. Think about what you could do for someone else that they would enjoy. It can be something as simple as a short love note and flower for a significant other or bringing a coffee for a valued co-worker. It's not the cost of what you do, it's the value that matters. What do I mean by that? Your thought and time have great value, much more than money.

Think about this example (paraphrased from Simon Sinek). If a friend came to work and said, "Hey, I just donated a dollar to a homeless guy on the way to work," how would you react?

What if they said they gave twenty dollars?

Now, what if that person came to work and said, "I spent one of my days off helping to clean up and paint an elementary school in the inner city." Wow. That expenditure of time has much more value than simply donating money.

Our time is valuable because it can't be replaced. That's why I donate my time teaching a class at a local ministry.

Think about how you can give some of your time to give back and make a difference in someone's life. I promise it'll be worth it.

Cheers!

Think about how you spend your time.

How often do you donate time to others?

_____

_____

_____

_____

How might it benefit you to help a charity?

_____

_____

_____

_____

How much time a month could you donate?

_____

_____

_____

_____

What local charity could you donate it to?

_____

_____

_____

_____

Follow your passion and you can change lives

We had another great session at The Overcomers ministry this evening. There were several new faces, which are always welcome. I made a change to the night's topic and played Nick Vujicic's video, *No Arms, No Legs, No Worries*. (For more information about Nick Vujicic visit his website at attitudeisaltitude.com.)

We also had a nice, though brief, open chat session. One participant asked me for some help with a personal issue. While I tried to offer some guidance, I told him ultimately he'd have to handle it himself and he can do it.

I get a lot from these sessions, and I trust they do, too. I would love to do more speaking engagements there (at least once a week), at youth centers, halfway houses, jails, and even prisons.

Everyone has the power within them to make positive change. Some of them just need to be shown how. Imagine reducing a state's recidivism rate by one, five or even 10 percent! Imagine the impact that would have. Fewer victims, less property damage, a reduction is criminal justice costs, etc.

I'm not naive enough to believe that everyone I speak to will make that change, but if I reach even one out of every 100 people I talk to, isn't it worth it? The ratio has been much better, thus far, both in the in-custody class I co-facilitated in the local jail and at The Overcomers ministry where I volunteer my time. I love connecting with others and sharing what I've learned. Like I tell my class, my goal is to introduce them to simple ideas that can radically change their lives.

My goal is to introduce them to simple ideas that can radically change their lives.

Following my passion has already changed mine.

Think about your passion.

What gets you excited each day?

_____

_____

_____

If money were no object, what would you do?

_____

_____

_____

What's a simple act from someone else that you're grateful for?

_____

_____

_____

How can one act of kindness from you affect someone else's life?

_____

_____

_____

Why you should keep an organizer

Not long ago I learned a very valuable lesson about the importance of maintaining an organizer or appointment book. I bought an organizer not long ago after hearing several highly successful people talk about how important they were. You could say my mentors were telling me to "Get an organizer!" So I did.

The first week I was diligent about documenting my appointments and the various important things on my "To Do" list. A couple weeks later, however, I started slacking off a bit. I let "stinkin' thinkin'" creep into my head and I accepted some lame old excuses for not maintaining it. You're probably familiar with the excuses. They include:

- I'll remember that
- I'll write it in the organizer later
- I'm too tired to get to it right now

You've probably guessed how this story turns out. After a couple of weeks, I made the decision to get back on track and start using the organizer more diligently. I opened it up to see what appointments I had coming up. As I looked down onto the page covering a previous week I realized I had missed an appointment!

I don't need to tell you that missing an appointment not only isn't professional but it can down right destroy your credibility with the prospective client (or partner). I felt completely ashamed and stupid. If I had just followed the simple advice of other successful people I would have made the appointment and I might have signed one more customer. As it is, my poor choices have forced me into "damage control" mode.

The moral of the story: Do the simple things that will lead to success. That includes buying and maintaining an organizer!

Consider your daily schedule.

How important is it to be well organized?

_____

_____

_____

_____

Do you organize events in your life?

_____

_____

_____

Do you use a traditional organizer or an electronic device (smart phone, tablet)?

_____

_____

_____

What are some things besides appointments you could put in an organizer?

_____

_____

_____

_____

How to get more out of life

Don't discount the impact you have on others. Even in difficult times, a single word of encouragement can change someone's life. Something that comes as second nature to you can make a radical difference to another person.

Oprah Winfrey once wrote, "One of the defining moments of my life came in fourth grade—the year I was a student in Mrs. Duncan's class at Wharton Elementary School in Nashville. For the first time, I wasn't afraid to be smart, and she often stayed after school to work with me. ... As a child, I hadn't even considered that Mrs. Duncan might have had a life beyond our class. It was in her class that I really came into myself. After all these years, I could say thank you to a woman who had a powerful impact on my early life."

Whether in your professional life, personal life or spiritual life, be cognizant of the way you treat people, of the way you react to situations. Don't strive solely for your own success but strive to help someone else, as well.

The result can't be measured nor the reward collected at the time of the transaction. The true value is revealed days, months or even years later when someone you've impacted impacts another person's life – or many lives. As Darren Hardy, author of *The Compound Effect*, says, "Small actions add up to positive results."

The "butterfly effect" is real. I'm planting the seeds because I believe in people. Great people have left their mark on me. Many have no idea of their impact on my life. A school teacher, a deputy sheriff, an NFL player, a public speaker, a family member… I can never repay any of them for the positive effect they had on me as a human being, so I'm focusing on paying it forward, on investing in myself and others.

One of the passions I have discovered is working with people who have placed themselves in "undesirable circumstances" due to their choices. As Jim Rohn would say in his trademark voice, "They messed up!" Helping them to think differently, to see different possibilities and options, and to start making better choices is something I believe in.

Over the past three years I co-developed a gang diversion class for in-custody adults. The program finally got funded and I spent several months co-facilitating the class to inmates. I witnessed the dramatic change that some of them went through in those three months. Unfortunately, my time there came to an end and I was moved on to another area. Later, I learned that some of the inmates have been asking for me to come back to the program.

I knew we had reached some of them, but it seems I made a bigger impact on some than I expected. Regardless of whether I work with that program again, I hope they'll carry that further and turn something good into something great, and make choices that will keep them off the path of incarceration and onto the path of a successful life "outside" of the system. It feels good knowing that at least some of them see their own potential and may do just that.

Do you want to know how to get more out of life? Do you want to improve areas of your own life? If the answer is yes to either question, then find ways to enrich the lives of others. The more you give (of yourself) the more you will receive in life.

Think about the importance of mentors.

Who would you thank today, if you could?

_____

_____

_____

_____

Who has had a positive impact on your life?

_____

_____

_____

_____

Who could you add value to in your life?

_____

_____

_____

_____

Name three ways you could 'pay it forward'?

_____

_____

_____

_____

To reach your goals, insist you persist

Some time ago I was reassigned to a different position at my job. As a result, I was unable to continue facilitating an in-custody gang diversion and mindset class that I co-developed. At the time it seemed that I wouldn't be able to teach the class again. That door was closed and it was completely beyond my control. But that wasn't the end.

I am a student of some incredibly successful people and every one of them has something to say about what to do when obstacles crop up on your journey to success. You've heard the saying, 'Anything worth having is worth working for,' right? Well, my mentors have taught me that anything worth having will take hard work, that showing up is 50% of success, and the other 50% is persistence!

So I kept at it. I kept my vision of speaking to groups of people and of introducing them to concepts and ideas that could change their lives, if only they would apply what they learned. I kept looking for opportunities to reach my goal. Those opportunities appeared. Because I set my mind right, I recognized the for what they were and took action.

A few weeks back I went to a *Success* symposium that was held at a local church. A short time later I had a conversation with the director of a program associated with that same church. The program is designed to help former drug addicts and prisoners get back on their feet, teach them life skills, provide spiritual guidance, and redirect their lives. I asked the director if he would consider allowing me to speak to the participants of his program. He enthusiastically accepted (he'd witnessed me facilitate my previous class and saw the results first hand).

Thus began the administrative process of getting my class arranged and scheduled. We settled on every other Wednesday night. The first start date (earlier this month) had to be postponed due to a scheduling conflict. The new start date would be March 20th.

So last night I taught my first class ("facilitated" might be a better word.) I was anxious and a little nervous but it went as well — if not better — than I expected. The staff and participants were receptive and open to hearing my message. It was interactive and my audience was engaged. They listened, intently watched the video I showed them (a powerful one by Eric Thomas; if you haven't heard of him yet, you will), and they asked questions.

By the end of my hour at the program I felt a sense of accomplishment and fulfillment. I had shared my vision and the ideas I'd learned from others, and I reached someone (in this case, it seems, everyone). Then I got a bonus. Every one of the men in the class came up to me, shook my hand, and thanked me for coming. One young man asked me if there was any way I could come more often, and asked if I would be willing to come out on visit day in the event his family couldn't make it to visit him. That made a strong impression on me.

I don't mention those things to toot my own horn. For me it was about the feeling I got knowing that I had reached those people in the audience, that perhaps they now have a little more inspiration to aim higher and accomplish more. I feel good knowing that I gave something more valuable than money — I gave my time — and it was appreciated.

I knew I was doing the right thing and for the right reasons.

Most people have written these people off, and not without reason. But the people in this program want to change their lives. Just by being in the program they have taken action, which puts them in the small percentage of people that we call "successful."

Pastor Joel Osteen, of Lakewood Church, said in an interview, "I like to tell people there are seeds of greatness on the inside of every person. ... You can make a great difference in our world. ... God uses ordinary people to do extraordinary things."

I want to make a difference — I *am* making a difference — in the lives of the people I'm reaching. On that level, I'm already a success. My long-term goal, however, is much bigger. I want to speak to prison and jail populations and reach as many "throw-a-ways" as possible and help as many of these people as possible find their inner potential to be successful in life.

I decided back in October that I wasn't going to allow anyone else to define me nor to stand in the way of my dream. I have a message to share. I will make a difference in people's lives. I know that God wouldn't put that dream in my heart if it wasn't meant for me to pursue. As long as I remain in faith, stay true to myself, and keep moving toward my goal, one day I will achieve it.

Yesterday proved that to me.

Think of a dream you have.

Have you been working toward this dream?

_____

_____

_____

_____

What would be the result of giving up?

_____

_____

_____

_____

What will you gain when you succeed?

_____

_____

_____

_____

Write an inspirational quote to encourage you to keep working toward your dream:

_____

_____

_____

_____

Act your way to success

It's one thing to come to the realization that you want things to be different. That moment when you realize that things aren't all they're cracked up to be. Maybe you're unhappy with being in a stagnant career or looking at a personal relationship and wishing it were more fulfilling. That moment when we recognize that something has to change in order for us to be happier can be powerful. There's another side of that coin, however.

The late, great Jim Rohn said, "For things can change, we need to change." Making that decision that we want something to change is a step but merely wishing for something is a dream. While dreaming is good, a desire that isn't acted upon remains simply a wish. The next step in the process is turning thought into action. But how do we do that?

"A desire that isn't acted upon remains simply a wish."

I wrestled with this question recently. After starting my own business, I had the roadmap to success laid out for me by others who had already achieved great success with the same company I was working with. There was no question that I had everything they had. I had the same tools, the same marketing materials, the same products and services to sell, access to the same training, and so on. What makes the difference between their level of success and my own?

"Should" Happens

Most of us know what we should do to get what we want (at least if you've done any kind of study or research into how to reach your goal). If we want to become more physically fit, we need to exercise more. Therefor we should exercise. If we want to be more successful in our chosen career we need to expand our skillset, our contacts, and our overall value in the market place. We should do those things. We all know what we should do. International speaker Anthony Robbins says that often times we "should all over ourselves." He's got a valid point.

I knew I should do the things necessary to see success in my business but the motivation needed to move myself to action was lacking. My "should" was not yet a "must," as Robbins says. I had to reflect and honestly evaluate why I was frozen (because that's what I was). I knew – I believed – with every fiber of my being that I wanted the results and I needed the results. So why wasn't I taking action?

The Grip of Fear

If you're not doing what you know you need to do – if your "should" is not yet a "must," it could be for any of a number of reasons. But often it simply comes down to fear. Fear of the unknown is a powerful distractor. Often the known, even a painful or uncomfortable one, is difficult to let go of when the alternative is the unknown. "Maybe the alternative is even worse," we tell ourselves.

Perhaps it's fear of speaking to strangers or people we know, or speaking before groups. Perhaps it's a fear of success. All the images of luxury cars, expensive homes, and the like, can't always override the comfort that the known gives us. Perhaps we don't feel as though we deserve success, no matter how much we want it. (That's hooey, by the way; you do deserve success.) Whatever the reason and whatever the form, fear can create a huge wall between us and our goals. Don't let fear stand between you and success.

Think about a change you want in life.

Name a "should" that needs to be a "must":

_____

_____

_____

_____

How would life be different if you made the change?

_____

_____

_____

_____

List three things that can help you to make the transition:

_____

_____

_____

_____

Set a deadline (date) to make the change:

_____

_____

To overcome fear, you must act

So how do we overcome that fear to do the things we need to do to be successful? It comes down to two things.

First, as I mentioned earlier, our "should" needs to become our "must." There can be no doubt that we must do the things required for success if we are to have success. There is no question. Our motivation must be so strong that the alternative (not taking action) is inconceivable. We must not just want something. We must seek it out with all the passion and conviction that's inside of us.

"Our motivation must be so strong that the alternative (not taking action) is inconceivable."

Motivational speaker Eric Thomas tells a story with the lesson "Until you want success as bad as you want to breathe, you won't be successful." That's powerful. If you think about it, wanting something so badly that you will do anything to achieve it virtually guarantees success. No matter what it takes, no matter how long it takes, you will have it. That needs to be your mindset.

Once you have the desperate, burning desire that turns your "should" into a "must," the second part is easy. Take action. Without belief, desire dies on the vine. It's the law of diminishing intent. The longer we go without acting on an idea, the less likely we are to ever see it to reality. You may have heard people say "Leaders act." Considering ramifications is fine but endless analysis leads to paralysis. There comes a point when you simply have to act.

"Any leader who's honest with you will tell you that before they became great they were just good."

That was the difference between me and the others who had achieved success in my business. They took action. That's not to say that they didn't stumble at first. Any leader who's honest with you will tell you that before they became great they were just good. In order to become good, they had to rise from mediocrity. Before they were mediocre they more than likely sucked at what they were doing. It's the same in any endeavor.

Think about your first day at a new job or a new school. You didn't know what you were doing, you didn't know anyone, and you didn't know your way around. Let's face it. You were less than mediocre! But eventually you got good at it. You got to know people and you even made new friends. You learned your way around so well that you could show up and navigate your way around while reading a book and drinking coffee at the same time! So it is with any new endeavor.

Find Your Why

Allow me to sum up this entire piece of writing very succinctly. To be successful you must have a burning desire that compels you to act despite any fears. If you do this, you will overcome the fear. The unknown becomes routine and, by continuing to take action, you will go from mediocre to good and eventually to great.

Am I a business guru? Not by any stretch. Have I made mistakes? Absolutely. Those mistakes and failures are the very reason I am getting better and better each day.

Nobody promised me an easy path. They merely gave me a map. The journey is mine to take or not. I choose to take it. If you take it, too, you can read the notes I'm leaving along the way so you know what to expect. That should make your journey a little easier.

Here's to your success!

Think of an important goal you have.

Why is the goal important to you?

_____

_____

_____

_____

What are you willing to sacrifice to reach it?

_____

_____

_____

_____

List one action you can take daily toward reaching your goal?

_____

_____

_____

List three smaller goals that will lead to your big goal:

_____

_____

_____

_____

Give up or press on?

The longer you've lived the more setbacks you'll likely be able to recall in your life. Nearly everyone can recall at least one time when something they'd worked hard for disappeared or was taken away. It could be a coveted position at your workplace, a special accomplishment on a sports team (such as winning a championship or breaking a record), or even a relationship you thought was "the one." The commonality is that it was something that was supposed to endure. Like the proverbial sandcastle on the beach, however, life has a way of coming along and tearing things down.

So what's the point of putting in effort when everything seems hopeless? What's the point of pressing on when the success you have already achieved is ripped away from you? What's the point, indeed?

The answer is simple and may seem trite but here it is. You continue on because what appears to be the end isn't. You see? Simple. That's hardly sufficient to assuage the anger, sadness and despair that some people feel when faced with a great loss, I know. Therein lies the rub. It's not supposed to.

When we accept that life is full of setbacks, that it will constantly beat us down, we have only two choices; give up or press on. Too many people choose to give up and this is because they don't see anything in their future. They believe that what they have accomplished – perhaps the best they've ever done – as the best they will ever do. This is the self-limiting thought that kills dreams.

The reality is that as human beings we are capable of much, much more than we realize. Exceptional sports comebacks, feats of superhuman prowess in emergencies, miraculous cures, and so on, happen with enough frequency that they cannot be denied. Amazing things do happen. Individuals just like you and me accomplish amazing things and yet we believe that we are not cut of the same cloth. So we take great pride in our own accomplishments and put them on a pedestal and beam with pride, for we could never accomplish a greater feat in our lives! That's a lie we tell ourselves to add value on what we have done and to give us permission not to try harder, to risk failure, so that we can achieve more.

Human beings thrive on challenge and adversity but many of us do not like pain. In fact, we do almost anything to avoid it. Many of us fear it. Except when we believe we must do something, in which case suddenly the pain becomes almost irrelevant, the cost of our efforts outweighed by the fact that the thing must be done. To quote one of my mentors, "When the 'Why' is big enough, the 'How' doesn't matter."

To borrow an example from Darren Hardy, imagine being offered twenty dollars to walk across a 100-foot metal beam that is resting on the ground. No problem. We could easily walk the beam because there is no real risk to us and the benefit or gain is an easy twenty dollars. Next imagine the beam is resting atop and bridging two tall skyscrapers and we are offered the same twenty dollars to walk across the beam. Most people would say "No way!" because the risk far outweighs the benefit.

Now imagine standing atop one of the buildings with your young child on the far building, which is engulfed in flames, and only by crossing the beam can they be saved. We would do it in a heartbeat to save our child, regardless of the money! Why? Because our reason, our "Why" is a *must* and far outweighs the risk.

When we accomplish something great in our lives we feel proud of our accomplishment. If that accomplishment is undone or taken away, however, we may feel defeated but we shouldn't. Time changes everything. Nothing is untouched by time. In our dream position we will eventually become stagnant or "comfortable" and stop pushing ourselves. We're no longer growing and no longer doing our best in that position. Athletic records will one day be broken and the next year brings a new round of playoffs and (usually) a new champion. Relationships change over time and sometimes "the one" turns out not to be the one after all.

What we need to realize is that there is more. There is always more. More to be tried, more to be gained, more to be learned, and more potential to be realized. This is one of the lessons that needs to be learned for more personal growth to occur.

As the great Jim Rohn once said, "Every life form seems to strive to its maximum except human beings. How tall will a tree grow? As tall as it possibly can. Human beings, on the other hand, have been given the dignity of choice. You can choose to be all or you can choose to be less. Why not stretch up to the full measure of the challenge and see what all you can do?"

Too many people reach a certain point and are content to stay there, not giving themselves permission to grow further, to experience more, to be more. When something great comes to an end, we need to remember that all things come to an end. An accomplishment of any kind should be viewed as a milestone, not a Stop sign. Hope is essential. We should maintain faith that we are destined for great things if we simply continue the work.

Don't be satisfied with quitting after your accomplishment. Compete against yourself to best your best! Don't sit on your laurels after setting a record. Work harder and beat your own record! Don't believe for a second that a relationship that ends is all you were meant to have. Know that the relationship ended to make way for a better relationship that is truly meant for you!

"What you think is a setback, is really a set-up for a greater comeback!" – Joel Osteen

It's not how many times we get knocked down in life. It's how many times we get back up again. The definition of success is getting up one more time than you get knocked down. So stop feeling sorry for yourself and press on! Use your setback as a launching pad to get up and get back at it. You will achieve what you set out to and then some. When it's all said and done you'll look back and be glad you didn't settle, that you didn't quit, and it will feel darned good.

Think of a recent setback you faced.

What is a positive thing that did (or could) result from the setback?

_____

_____

_____

_____

What need was left unfulfilled (love, acceptance, recognition, etc.)?

_____

_____

_____

_____

Name another way you could fill that need.

_____

_____

_____

Name a time you didn't quit. How did it feel?

_____

_____

_____

_____

The odds of success

A recent discussion about "the odds of success" led to some interesting statistics as well as a real reality check. People who declare a dream or seemingly outlandish goal are often told, "Do you know the odds of you doing that?" If you've ever attempted something outside the so-called norm, you've no doubt heard something similar. The point of the objection (as though their opinion really mattered) is that the "odds" of you accomplishing your stated goal are so low you might as well not even try because you're virtually guaranteed to fail.

Well, before I address that objection let's look at those statistics I mentioned.

- Getting pregnant from a one-night stand: 1 in 20
- Getting struck by lightning: 1 in 10,000
- Dying in an airplane crash: 1 in 355,318
- Being dealt a royal flush in a given hand of poker: 1 in 655,750
- Dying from flesh-eating bacteria: 1 in 1 million
- Winning the California Super Lotto Jackpot: 1 in 18 million.

Those are some pretty outlandish odds, right? Well, now for the reality check.

The truth is that your achieving a goal is not a matter of chance, it's a matter of persistence and determination. Think about it. If you want something bad enough and work at it long enough, you can achieve it.

The legendary author Napoleon Hill once said, "What the mind can conceive and believe it can achieve, regardless of how many times you may have failed in the past or how lofty your hopes may be."

The "odds of success" don't predetermine your likelihood of achieving their dream. All the "odds" tell you is how many people gave up on theirs! Network marketing professional Tim Sales calls the "odds" claim an irrelevant one. He explains it this way:

"If I want to get fit, what are the odds that I actually will?" Huh? That seems like an irrelevant question, doesn't it? Why? Because 'odds' have nothing to do with me getting off the couch and tossing the potato chips in the trash. 'Odds' are incorrectly used when performance can alter the odds."

He goes on to use the example of rolling a die. There's no "performance" involved, and the odds are one in six of its landing on any given number. Likewise, flipping a coin has a fifty percent chance of coming up "heads." It's the same thing when you buy a lottery ticket (that's my clever association with the photo image at the start of this article). The 'odds' come in to play because there is absolutely no skill or performance involved that can affect the outcome.

On the other side of the proverbial coin, playing golf (or any other sport) involves performance. When you're building a business performance is involved, as well, and "odds" are irrelevant. Like Tim Sales says,

That's how any person gets better at any skill or skill set. Your actions and results dictate whether you achieve your goals. Nothing else matters. In Anthony Robbins' seminars he teaches the audience to internalize and maintain a positive strength, by declaring loudly:

"Now *I* am the voice! I will *lead*, not follow. I will *believe*, not doubt. I will *create*, not destroy! I am a force for good. I am a leader! Defy the odds! Set a new standard! *Step up!*"

Now that's a powerful affirmation! It also reinforces the point that the odds are irrelevant. Once we decide and believe in our minds that we can and will achieve something, and take action on those beliefs, we set the odds. Nothing else matters.

So the next time someone tells you that the odds are against you achieving your goals, look them in the eye and tell them "odds" have nothing to do with it. Another way to put might be to say, "I set the odds."

Thinking about the odds.

Name a time you succeeded when you "should have" failed:

_____

_____

_____

List things you do as part of a daily routine:

_____

_____

_____

_____

List something you would try if you *knew* you absolutely *could not* fail.

_____

_____

_____

Name something you're committed to where you absolutely refuse to accept defeat:

_____

_____

_____

How to receive more

How can you receive more in your life? To receive more, you have to *give* more. As Thanksgiving passes by us and we consume countless variations of meals comprised of turkey, potatoes and stuffing, I'm left thinking about the meaning of the holiday. Not about what that day meant for me but about what it means for me today. Is life about the effort to receive more? Quite the contrary.

The name itself is made up of two words: "thanks" and "giving." Sure, on the surface it means to give thanks (presumably for blessings in your life or other things worthy of thanks) but one of those two words means more to me today than it did last Thursday — Giving.

Some great minds have espoused the belief that in order to receive something you first have to give it. It's one of the "laws" of success. Think about that for a minute. In order to receive something from someone you first have to give that thing to someone else. Do you want to receive more smiles from strangers? Than give more smiles to strangers. Do you want to receive more praise? Then give more praise to others. Do you want to be honored? Then honor someone else. Do you want to receive more financial success? Then help someone else to achieve financial success.

Rita Davenport, a successful public speaker, said "Never leave a hotel without tipping the maid who cleans your room." There's great wisdom in that simple statement. Some people may wonder "How much should you tip the maid?" Ms. Davenport asks how much you would tip the maid if it were your own baby girl, or sister or wife who was the maid?

In the book titled *The Go-Giver, A Little Story About A Powerful Business Idea*, by Bob Burg and John David Mann, the fictional character Pindar tells a struggling salesman, "Most people just laugh when they hear that the secret to success is giving…Then again, most people are nowhere near as successful as they wish they were." How true.

Providing something extra to someone, whether it's extra money, honor, praise, a smile, or something else, is a simple gift. It's a gift that can help that person in ways that you can't comprehend. It could mean putting dinner in their children's stomachs. It could mean putting a smile on their face that had been absent all day long. It could mean increasing their sense of self-worth. It could mean giving them hope when they need it most. John C. Maxwell calls it adding value to others. It's a powerful ability and it is crucial for your success.

So the next time you find yourself wanting something, wanting more, think about how you can give to someone else. In fact, think about three things you want to receive today and then think of three people you can give those things to. Switch your mindset from being a "go-getter" to being a "go-giver." As you develop a sense of gratitude and giving you will advance your journey to success.

Take a moment to think about gratitude.

Name some things you're grateful for:

_____

_____

_____

_____

What is a way you can bring joy to someone in your life or someone you see daily?

_____

_____

_____

_____

Write "Thank you" three times.

_____

_____

_____

Name something you want more of, then write the name of someone you'll give that to.

_____

_____

_____

Don't walk backwards

"In order to grow you have to get outside your comfort zone." I've heard that said many times and in many ways. The words are sometimes different but the message is the same. One of the best was Jim Rohn, who addressed this issue in many seminars. He once said,

"Most people are seduced by the lure of the comfort zone. This can be likened to going out of a warm house on a cold, windy morning. The average person, when he feels the storm swirling outside his comfort zone, rushes back inside where it's nice and warm. But not the true leader. The true leader has the courage to step away from the familiar and comfortable and to face the unknown with no guarantees of success. It is this ability to 'boldly go where no man has gone before' that distinguishes you as a leader from the average person. This is the example that you must set if you are to rise above the average. It is this example that inspires and motivates other people to rise above their previous levels of accomplishment as well."

Each of us has a comfort zone. It's that place or that activity or that situation in which we feel safe. Very little can shake our confidence when we're there. We become comfortable. We become complacent. Only when we go outside and into that swirling storm does our mettle become truly tested, does adversity threaten us. Only when our resources become less meaningful do we have to draw deeper for resources we may have forgotten we had or seek out new ones. Only when we are uncomfortable do we learn how much we can truly endure. And in that enduring we can find new strength.

Not long ago I was in a "dream" position at my job. I had been there for five years and actually helped create the position. I cherished my office partners and I thrived in the position. I was challenged almost daily and was able to expand my knowledge on topics that I found quite interesting. I was engaged. I had value. And for a time I was appreciated.

The last year or so I felt less valued. I was less engaged. The job was quite as thrilling as it once was. I was getting comfortable. But I found new challenges in that position. I found new ways to stay busy, specialty topics to learn about. I was content. I was comfortable.

I decided to take a healthy vacation with my family, something I hadn't done in years. I had a wonderful time. I visited places of natural beauty, reconnected with family we hadn't seen in years. I was refreshed. Recharged. I came back to work and things felt all right. I had a new goals and new aspirations that were reinforced by my change in perspective from that vacation.

Then one day I was told that my position was being cut. I was to move out of the office I'd occupied for years and return to an old assignment I had. The reason for the decision is unimportant. The decision was made and I had to figure out what I was going to do. I was certainly outside my comfort zone. I felt confused and upset at first, but only for a short time. When I looked at my situation and realized I couldn't change it I started looking for benefits. How could I benefit from the change? What opportunities lay ahead of me now that I'd moved out into the swirling storm?

One thing was for certain; I decided not to waste any time dwelling on the past, on what was and why things happened the way they did. I likened that to walking through life backwards, always looking at what had already passed. I realized that if I did that I would miss every single opportunity that came along, seeing it only as it went by me. I realized I needed to look ahead, to be open to new possibilities, new opportunities as they approached me so that I could recognize them and take advantage of them before they slipped by me.

What's happening in your life that has put you outside of your comfort zone? How do you react when it happens? Do you start walking backwards, bemoaning your loss and wondering how to get it back? Or do you walk forward, acknowledging what happened but look toward the future, keeping your eyes open for new opportunities?

Look ahead. Have faith that yesterday's negative events don't determine your future unless you walk backward. Learn from your mistakes and from things that happen to you so that you can avoid them in the future. Walk facing forward. It's the only way you can steer your life toward success.

Think about a recent loss or mistake.

What is a lesson you could take from it?

_____

_____

_____

_____

_____

What can you do different to avoid such a loss or mistake in the future?

_____

_____

_____

_____

_____

How can you share your experience to help someone else?

_____

_____

_____

_____

_____

What Bob Ross taught me about success

Today is the birthday of Bob Ross, the soft-spoken man with the afro who taught millions how to paint trees on *The Joy of Painting*, which ran on PBS from 1983 to 1994. Mr. Ross passed away of lymphoma in 1995 but he is remembered by millions as the kind man with the gentle voice, even by those who didn't watch his program regularly.

There are some things that not many people know about Mr. Ross, some of which I just learned today. For example, he was a Non-commissioned Officer (NCO) in the United States Air Force, retiring after 20 years of service at the rank of Master Sergeant. The most striking thing about his career as an artist and business man, however, was how much money he made doing *The Joy of Painting*. Guess how much money he made?

Nothing. He made *no* money from PBS for a program that ran for nearly twelve years!

"How can this be," you ask? "Why would he work for free?" Because he was a very smart man who understood success. You see, he made his income from Bob Ross, Inc., his company through which he sold art supplies, instructional videotapes, taught classes, "and even had a troupe of traveling art instructors who roamed the world teaching painting." The television program was merely a vehicle for building his brand — namely his name and face (and hair)!

Ross, it turns out, recorded those programs nearly as quickly as he created his artwork. According to mentalfloss.com, "Ross could bang out an entire 13-episode season of The Joy of Painting in just over two days, which freed him up to get back to teaching lessons."

In short, he gave to his audience before they became his customers. Ross contributed to the art community in the best (and most rewarding) way possible — by attracting people to it. His instruction, his personality, and his soft voice attracted people to him and, ultimately, to his business.

This "attraction marketing" can work for you and I, as well. By providing something of value to others for free, by giving to others, others come to know us and (hopefully) trust us. That, in turn, will attract them to us and do business with us. By giving to others you will no doubt receive. It's important to note, however, that in giving you cannot expect anything in return. That's how trust is gained.

Think about your occupation or business.

How could you provide more value to your customers or clients?

_____

_____

_____

_____

What are some potential benefits of providing more value to others?

_____

_____

_____

_____

How can you add more value to loved ones in your life?

_____

_____

_____

_____

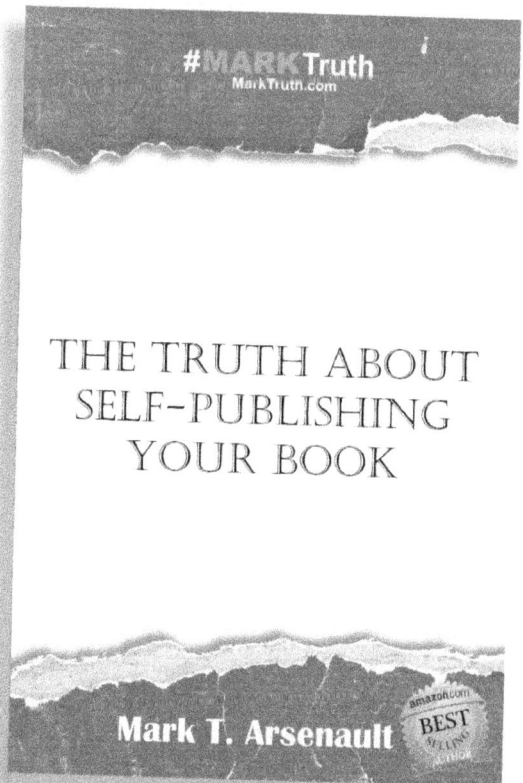

www.ingramcontent.com/pod-product-compliance
Lightning Source LLC
Chambersburg PA
CBHW071609040426
42452CB00008B/1296